W9-AFR-361

Stretching Ourselves

Kids with Cerebral Palsy

Alden R. Carter

PHOTOGRAPHS BY *Carol S. Carter*

Albert Whitman & Company • Morton Grove, Illinois

Library of Congress Cataloging-in-Publication Data

Carter, Alden R.
Stretching ourselves: kids with cerebral palsy /
by Alden R. Carter;
photographs by Carol S. Carter.
        p. cm.
        Summary: Describes cerebral palsy and focuses on
the daily lives of three children with varying degrees of
this condition.
        ISBN 0-8075-7637-9
        1. Cerebral palsy—Juvenile literature. 2. Cerebral
palsied children—Juvenile literature. [1. Cerebral palsy.]
I. Carter, Carol S., ill. II. Title.

RJ496.C4 C36 2000
362.1'9892836—dc21
                                99-040085

The design is by Pamela Kende.
The text typeface is Caslon.

About the Author and Photographer

Alden R. Carter is the author of more than
thirty books for children and young
adults, including the celebrated novels
Up Country, *Dogwolf*, *Between a Rock
and a Hard Place*, and *Bull Catcher*.
With his daughter, Siri, he wrote *I'm
Tougher than Asthma!*, an *American
Bookseller* "Pick of the Lists."

Carol S. Carter is a graduate of the Rocky
Mountain School of Photography.
Her work has appeared in several
previous books by her husband, Alden,
including *Big Brother Dustin*, *Dustin's
Big School Day* (both with Dan Young),
and *Seeing Things My Way*.

The Carters live in Marshfield, Wisconsin.

For Nic Campbell, Emily Eisberner, and Tanner Balz

~ Acknowledgments ~

Many thanks to all who helped with *Stretching Ourselves: Kids with Cerebral Palsy*, particularly Karen, Bob, Tony, Katie, Andrew, and Cheryl Eisberner; Cindy, Cory, and Cole Hoffman; Anthony Balz; Penny Campbell; Tami, Shylo, Chance, and Austin Whitlatch; Barb, Jerry, and Nicole Bryant; Jill, Leslie, and Leanna Martin; Tom Hilber; Greg Kucjek; Bob Johnson and Carol Park of the Gait Lab at the Marshfield Clinic, Marshfield, Wisconsin; Julie Johnson and her students at Stratford Elementary School, Stratford, Wisconsin; Sherri Bauer, Rae Fadrowski, Sharon Baumer, and their students at Grant Elementary School, Marshfield, Wisconsin; Jamie Skjeveland; Bev Shookman; Joan Doak; Alice Kapla; Kim Larson; Scott Scheuer; Lisa Berg; Katie Nelson; Megan Larson; Jason Douglas-Jones; Noah Shadis; Mike Ott; Cory Geldernick; Gale Bach; Brittany and Chris Snider; Georgia Staab; June Olson; and Rebecca Campbell, M.D. As always, our children, Brian and Siri, and our editor, Abby Levine, have our special gratitude.

Cerebral palsy is a disorder that affects the brain's control of voluntary muscles. The most common type is spasticity (extreme stiffness of muscles and tendons). Other types include choreoathetosis (uncontrolled flinging) and hypotonia (floppiness). In the United States, about two of every thousand children are born with some kind of CP. About five hundred thousand people in the U.S. have CP, making it the nation's most common developmental disorder.

The cause of a child's cerebral palsy is often mysterious. Surprisingly, birth injury results in fewer than 10 percent of all cases. The most common cause is "unknown," and other causes are so diverse and rare that their diagnosis can take years. This lack of explanation is only one of many emotional hurdles for families facing the challenges of cerebral palsy.

Cerebral palsy can be mild. Some children experience only a tightness in the ankles, a problem they may outgrow. It can also be severe, with profound impairment of motor control and problems with language, learning, swallowing, infection, and seizures. Although CP itself does not worsen, the strain put on muscles by growth and development can change the degree of disability. Hence, the evaluation and management of disabilities must be ongoing as the child matures.

For years we have talked of managing CP. But today there is a real possibility that we may soon be able to do more. Recent decades have brought significant improvement in the control of infection and seizures. Meanwhile, research has given us an understanding of the mechanisms of spasticity that may soon provide new treatments for this difficult condition.

Although we can look to the future with high hopes, we should remember that our most important tools already lie at hand. Every day, I see acceptance, optimism, and joy in my patients and their families. It is this courage in all its forms that provides the most potent and enduring means we have of meeting the daily challenges of life with cerebral palsy.

~ Rebecca Campbell, M.D. ~

∼ Resources ∼

The following organizations provide free or modestly priced books, pamphlets, videotapes, and educational programs:

National Easter Seal Society
230 W. Monroe St.
Suite 1800
Chicago, IL 60606
Phone: 312-726-6200
Web site: www.easter-seals.org

Children with Special Health Care Needs Program, Maternal and Child Health Bureau, Health Resources and Services Administration, U.S. Department of Health and Human Services
Parklawn Building
Room 6-05
5600 Fishers Lane
Rockville, MD 20857
Phone: 301-443-2350

United Cerebral Palsy Association, Inc.
1660 L Street NW
Suite 700
Washington, DC 20036
Phone (toll free): 800-872-5827
Web site: www.ucpa.org

Many wonderful books and magazines are available for the parents of children with cerebral palsy. Here are a few of the best:

Exceptional Parent Magazine
555 Kinderkamack Rd.
Oradell, NJ 07649
Phone (toll free): 877-372-7368

Finnie, Nancy. *Handling Your Young Cerebral Palsied Child at Home.* New York: Penguin U.S.A., 1970.

Geralis, Elaine, ed. *Children with Cerebral Palsy: A Parents' Guide.* Rockville, Md.: Woodbine House, 1991.

Miller, Freeman, and Steven Bachrach, et al., *Cerebral Palsy: A Complete Guide for Caregiving.* Baltimore: Johns Hopkins University Press, 1995.

Schleichkorn, Jay. *Coping with Cerebral Palsy: Answers to Questions Parents Often Ask.* Austin, Tex.: Pro Ed, 1993.

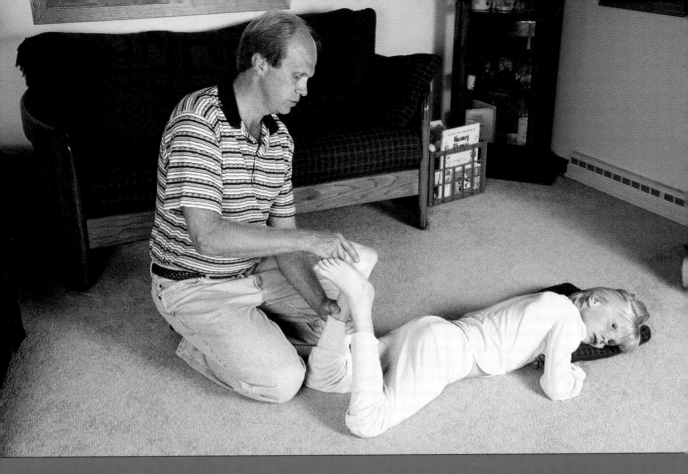

Bedtime always comes too soon at Emily's house. After snack and medicine, her dad helps her stretch her arms, hands, and legs. "Sassafras!" she growls. "Rhubarb!"

"You okay, Emmers?" he asks.

"Yep," Emily says, because even if stretching hurts, it helps her to move better.

Emily has cerebral palsy (CP). Most people with CP have tight muscles and tendons. Tendons are the thin, stretchy cords that connect muscles to bones. Our bodies move when muscles contract and relax, pulling or releasing tendons that move the bones of our arms, legs, hands, or spines. Stretching helps the muscles and tendons to work more freely.

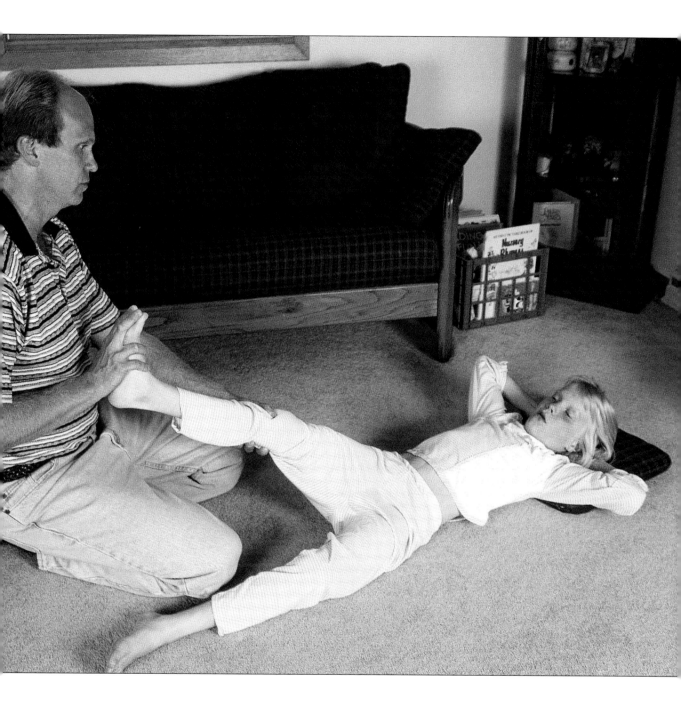

Emily has CP because her brain did not receive enough oxygen while she was in her mother's womb. The brain controls how we move, speak, see, smell, hear, and learn. People with CP can have trouble with any or all of these things. There is no cure for CP, and they must work hard to learn things that come easily to others. Emily practiced a whole summer with her mom and her brother Andrew, learning how to skate.

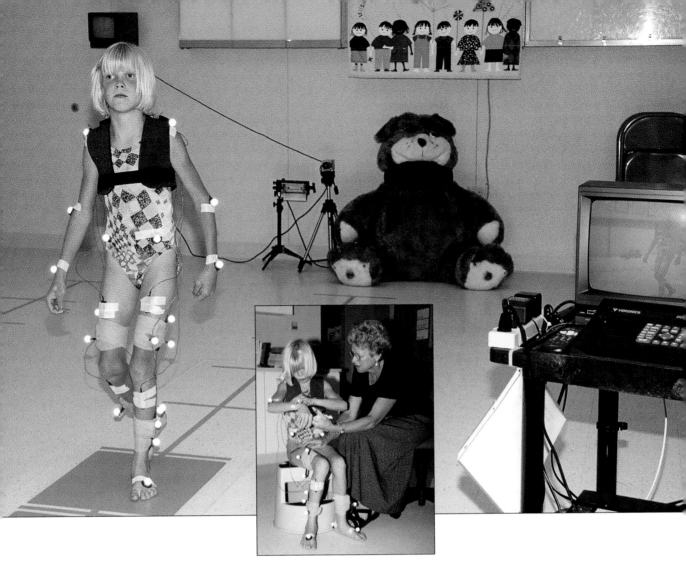

Because the muscles and tendons in her legs are tight, Emily's movements are stiff and she walks slightly bent forward. Twice a week, Emily's mom takes her to see a physical therapist. "I'm real bossy with my legs," she tells the therapist.

"That's good!" Ms. Park says. "But this morning, just relax. We're going to do a gait test to see how your legs are working with each other. Then we'll know the best exercises for you."

Emily's had operations on the muscles of her feet, bladder, and eyes. They've helped, but she's impatient. "Radishes!" she mutters, when she has to have another test to see how well her eyes are working together.

Emily's mom says, "Try again, sweetie."

"I'm not 'sweetie,' I'm *soury*," Emily says, but she has to grin.

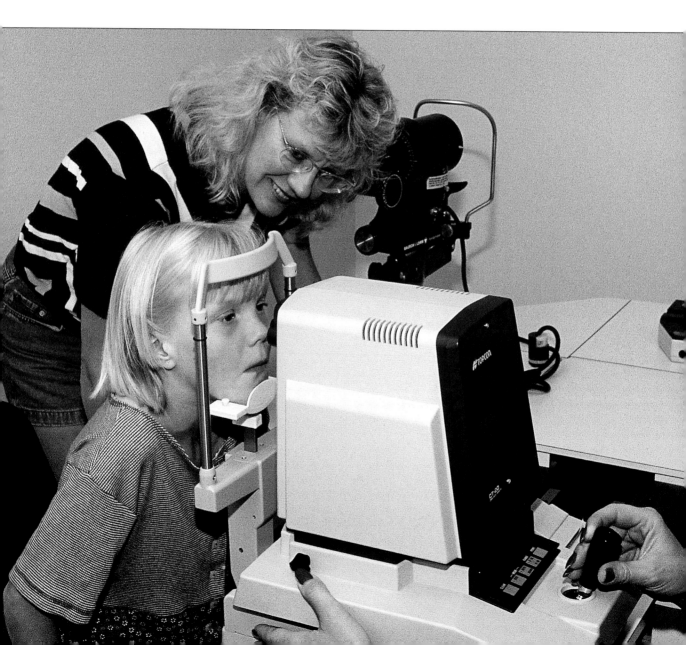

Having CP is tough. Emily used to get upset a lot. But she practices staying calm by mothering her dolls and caring for her dogs. Bole and Zuko don't always do what she wants, but she's learned to talk firmly instead of yelling.

Emily is crazy about basketball. Her brother Tony plays on a three-on-three basketball team. Her sister, Katie, is teaching Emily and two of her friends to be cheerleaders.

Emily likes playing even more than cheering, and between games she shoots some baskets with Jason. She thinks Jason is the cutest player on the team. Maybe someday they'll get married, but right now she just wants to beat him at H-O-R-S-E.

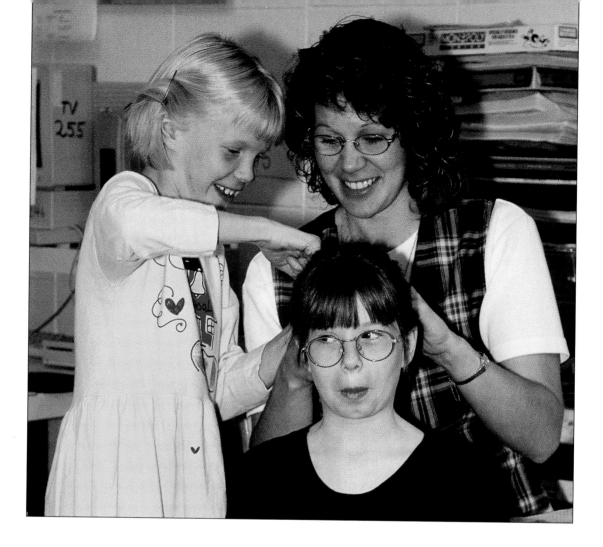

Cerebral palsy can affect how much and how fast a person can learn. Tasks that are simple for most people can be big challenges for people with CP. At school, Emily attends a special class for kids who need extra help. Today Mrs. Bauer is teaching them how to take better care of their hair, teeth, and skin. Emily grumbles about a snarl in Lizzy's hair.

"Celery!" Lizzy yelps.

"No vegetables!" Mrs. Bauer says. "Just keep at it. And, Emily, be gentle."

Emily also gets extra help for reading and math and then goes to regular classes for art, social studies, and music. She's especially good at art, and she never minds getting paint all over herself. "I'm like flowers and a rainbow!" she says.

Emily and Nic are friends at Grant School. Nic has CP because his brain was badly damaged during birth. He spends most of his time in a wheelchair and can speak only a few words. But no one likes playing ball, making jokes, or teasing the teachers more than Nic.

Every day Nic practices simple words with Ms. Larson, a speech therapist. She also helps him learn the buttons on his computer, which has an artificial voice. Nic's favorite button is "Give me a big bear hug!"

A lot of the other kids think his computer is pretty cool. At recess, Nic shows them how to use it. He makes it say "Let's play ball" and "Let's swing."

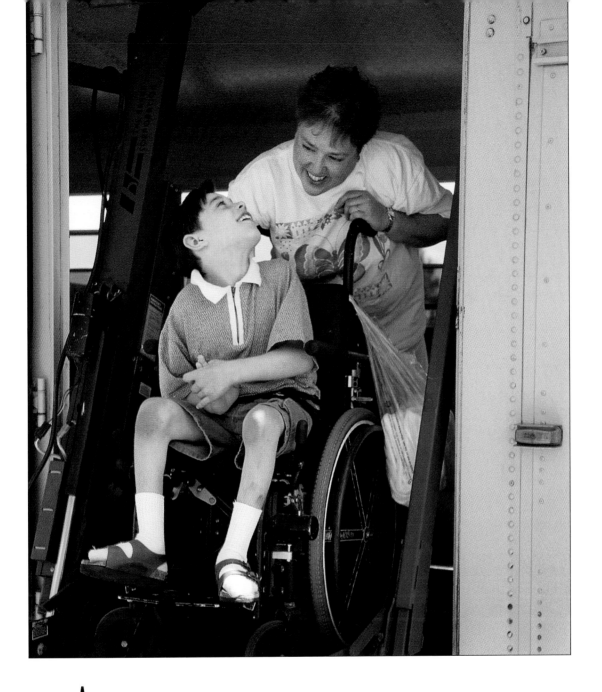

At the end of the school day, Nic rides the handicapped bus home. When Gale, his bus driver, starts the elevator, Nic likes to make crashing sounds. "Oh, my gosh, you're breaking the elevator again!" Gale yells.

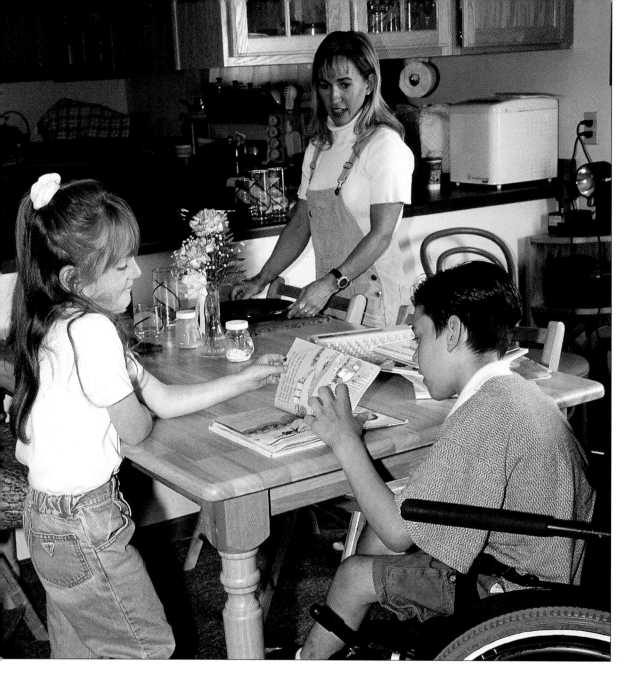

While his mom gets supper ready, Nic reads books with his cousin Shylo. Turning pages is good practice for his hands. He particularly likes books about bulldozers, farms, and football.

Nic, his mom, and his cousins go bowling some Friday nights. It's not easy for Nic because his hands won't always do what he wants them to do. When he gets a good roll, his mom yells, "Way to go, Nic!" And Nic's grin says everything he needs to say.

Just like at Emily's, bedtime always comes too soon at Nic's house. Nic and his mom add a few sentences to a letter for his dad, who is way across the ocean in the army. "Is there anything more you want to say?" his mom asks. Nic hugs himself, sending his dad a very big bear hug.

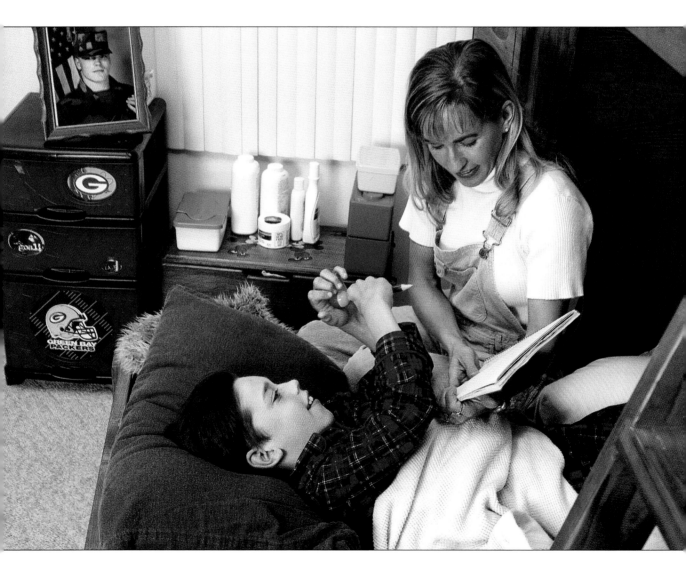

Saturdays are great days. At swimming class, Nic can kick, splash, and go under the water as much as he wants. (His mom yells if he does too much kicking, splashing, or diving in the bathtub.) "Lie back and relax, Tiger," Mr. Scheuer says. "We're going to practice floating."

Like Emily, Nic takes medicine for his CP. Last year, the doctors put a tiny pump in his abdomen. All day and all night, the pump delivers a small amount of medicine to help his muscles work better. Along with exercise and practice, the medicine may someday make it possible for Nic to walk on his own.

Nic feels loose after swimming. He practices with his walker. It's hard and frustrating. "Need some help, Nicky?" his mom calls. Nic shakes his head, growls "Self," and takes another step.

Tanner, too, would rather do things himself—even when they take longer. Tanner has milder CP than Nic or Emily, and many people don't notice his limp or his weak left arm. Tanner had bleeding in the brain—what's called a stroke— before he was born. Every day he practices to make his arm stronger and his fingers more nimble.

Tanner loves to play ball, especially football. "I'm going to be a fullback someday," he tells his brother, Anthony. "You bet!" Anthony says. "Just keep practicing."

Tanner is looking forward to having an operation to help his left arm. But first he must train it to move more freely. The doctors have given him a special brace to exercise his arm. "How does that feel?" his stepdad asks.

"Heavy, but I can handle it," Tanner says.

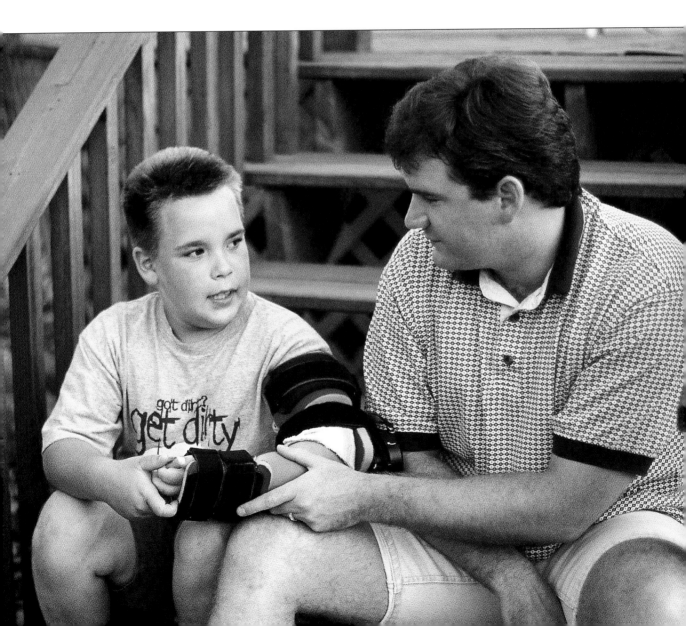

While his mom is busy, Tanner takes care of his new brother, Cole. "Slide the rings, Cole!" he tells him. Tanner could show him better using his right arm, but he practices using his left instead.

Tanner has a lot on his mind, and sometimes he falls behind in school. But he asks questions and gets help from friends. Pretty soon he's caught up again. "Arithmetic takes practice, practice, practice," Ms. Johnson tells the class.

"You bet!" Tanner says. After all, he knows lots about practicing.

o one in class—except maybe Ms. Johnson—reads stories better than Tanner. He does lots of different voices and can always make kids laugh. Next year maybe he'll try out for the football team *and* the school play.

Tanner loves recess. But sometimes friends shout "Hurry up, Tanner!" when he's already hurrying as fast as he can. And that makes him sad and a little mad.

But he remembers what his mom says: "You're way ahead on learning to be brave, Tanner."

People with CP *are* brave. Leslie Martin has had four operations for her CP. "Last time they sort of tossed me in a blender and poured a new kid out the other side," she likes telling people. Almost every Saturday, Leslie rides her horse, Annie. This summer she's going to teach Emily to ride.

"Ready to trot, Em?" she asks.

"You bet your broccoli!" Emily says.

Adults with CP work at many different jobs. Greg Kucjek, a friend of Tanner and his stepdad, schedules routes for a big fleet of trucks.

"Let me take it for a cruise, Greg," Tanner says.

Greg laughs. "In a few years, Tan my man."

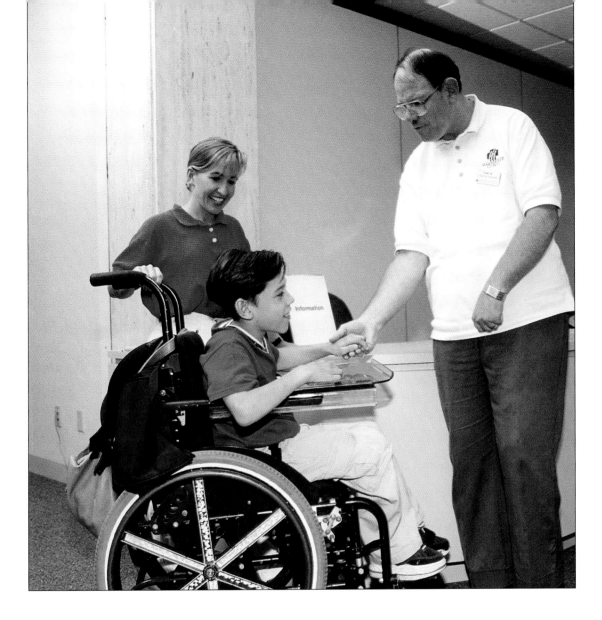

Tom Hilber, who works as a welcomer and guide at the Marshfield Clinic, is a special friend to Nic and a lot of kids who come to the clinic for help. "Give a five and you'll get a ten back every time," he often says. Like many people with CP, Tom is married. He and his wife, Jenny, have two grown children and two grandchildren.

Having CP means working hard at simple things. Tanner explains it this way: "Kids with CP are always trying. It can be tough when our bodies don't do what we want them to do. Some of us can't even talk to ask for something or to tell how we feel. But we keep working to do as much as we can."

Emily says, "Sometimes people are scared or shy because we move or talk funny. But you don't have to be. We like the same things you like. So, as Nic says—"

"Give us a big bear hug!"